In this book, we're going to talk about the amazing animal life in Australia and Oceania. So, let's get right to it!

There are seven continents in the world and Australia is the smallest continent. Australia as well as New Zealand and many other islands are part of the Oceania ecosystem.

Because these islands have been separated from other parts of the world for so long, and because they have so many unique habitats, their animals have evolved in a completely different way than other animals on Earth.

There are animals in Oceania that are not native anywhere else on Earth. A large portion of the land area is desert, but there are tropical rainforests as well. The Great Barrier Reef off the coast of Australia harbors unique sea life too.

An emu in the bushes.

The second largest bird in the world compared to the ostrich, the Australian emu is docile for the most part and very curious. Emus can't fly, but they are very fast runners and good swimmers. The male emu makes a sound that's like the sound of a pig. The female makes very loud booming sounds. Emus have very long necks and they have two eyelids on each eye. One eyelid is for blinking and the other is for keeping dust out.

Lone Emu standing on green grass.

Hector's Dolphin.

HECTOR'S DOLPHIN

The Hector's Dolphin is the smallest dolphin in the world. These dolphins are native to the coast off of New Zealand's North Island and they swim in the shallow waters. They grow to an average size of 4 feet long and they weigh about 110 pounds. Their faces have black markings and their dorsal fins resemble Mickey Mouse's ears. They use clicks as well as whistle sounds to communicate with each other. They're very curious, chase each other, and leap into the air. They've been seen playing with strands of seaweed.

Gecko on twigs.

JEWELED GECKO

Native to New Zealand, jeweled geckos are insectivores, which simply means that their diet is almost all insects. They have toes with long claws so they can climb the native trees and bushes of the forests and shrub lands where they live. Two different subgroups live in Otago as well as Canterbury. All of the geckos living in Otago are a bright green color and they have yellow and white patterns on their scales.

Some of the male geckos living in Canterbury have bodies that are brown or grey in color with white and purple scales. There are also geckos living on the South Island and they are green with no other markings. These interesting creatures are classified as an "at risk" group and are protected by law from capture or killing. They are one of the few species of geckos that give birth to live young.

Green Gecko.

Kangaroos jumping away.

KANGAROO

Kangaroos are native to Australia. There are four different species of *"Great Kangaroos,"* which are the largest types. They are the red kangaroo, the antilopine, the western gray, and the eastern gray. In addition to these species, there are also 12 species of smaller tree-sized kangaroos like the musky-rat kangaroo, which is only about 6 to 8 inches long and has a tail almost as long as its body.

Kangaroos are the only large animals on Earth that use hopping as their major way to move from one place to another. They can travel about 15 feet in just one hop. Their typical hopping speed is about 20 miles per hour, but they can travel as fast as 30 miles per hour.

They use their strong, muscular tails to help them push off the ground. They don't rush when they are foraging for food. They move more slowly and take their time.

Kangaroo in an open field.

Just like wombats and koalas, kangaroos are marsupials. The female kangaroos have pouches to carry their young. When born, the baby kangaroo, called a joey, can be as small as a single grain of rice! It may stay inside its mother's pouch for 120 to 450 days before it stops traveling with its mother. Kangaroos bring up their food and chew it a second time before it's digested just like cows do.

Newborn Kangaroo peaking out of Mother's Pouch.

Kiwi in bush.

KIWI

The kiwi is the National bird of New Zealand and the people of New Zealand are sometimes called "kiwis" too. Kiwis don't fly, but they can run quite fast. They have remnants of wings and very long malleable beaks. At the tips of their beaks they have nostrils and their ear openings are large.

Their legs are stout and muscular. They are nocturnal and come out at night to forage for food. Their diet consists of berries and small insects as well as insect larvae. During the daytime, they snooze in burrows. There are five species of kiwis and some are endangered.

Koala with baby, Hordern Vale, Australia.

KOALA BEAR

Native to Australia and found nowhere else in the wild, the koala bear has a very deceptive name. It's not a bear at all, instead, it's a cute, fuzzy marsupial with a nose that's shaped like a spoon and round, soft ears. Marsupials give birth to and carry their babies in a pouch. When the baby is born it only measures about 19 millimeters, which is about 7/10 of an inch. The baby koala stays hidden in its mother's pouch where it's protected for about half a year. When it finally comes out to see the world, it clings to its mother's back or her belly. It will go everywhere its mom goes until it's about a year old, then it will go off on its own.

Koalas sleep a lot. They sleep about 18 hours every day! They are nocturnal, which simply means that they are awake at night and asleep during the day. At night, they wake up so they can eat. Their primary diet is the leaves of eucalyptus trees. They will eat an average of about 1 kilogram of these leaves every single night. They can even save leaves in special cheek pouches so they can have a snack later on.

Koala bear in tree sleeping during the day.

Koalas have unique digestive systems that can handle the poisonous tough leaves and get nutrients from them. They eat so many leaves that they smell like eucalyptus cough drops! In order for koalas to survive they need a lot of space and about a hundred eucalyptus trees. As the woodlands of Australia continue to decrease, the koala's habitat will be at risk.

Young koala eating eucalyptus leaves.

Platypus swimming on the surface of a creek.

PLATYPUS

The platypus is hard to describe because it's very odd looking. It's semi-aquatic, which means it lives both on land and in the water. It has a bill like a duck, but it's a mammal. Unlike most mammals, it lays eggs. It has feet that look like an otter's and its tail resembles a beaver's tail. A native of eastern Australia and the island of Tasmania, the platypus is venomous and if you're stabbed by one of its spurs it's incredibly painful.

Close up of saltwater crocodile as emerges from water with a toothy grin.

SALTWATER CROCODILE

Called *"Salties"* by the Australians, the saltwater crocodile is the largest type of reptile on Earth. It's also one of the Earth's most dangerous predators and has a reputation as a maneater. It will stay underwater at the water's edge until its prey, either man or beast, stops to get some water or a drink.

Then, it explodes with force out of the water, grabs its victim in its jaws, and quickly drags it underwater until it drowns. These 23-foot long reptiles weigh over 2,000 pounds. They are deadly on land and in the water, but they can also go into hibernation on land and move so slightly that they appear to be dead themselves.

Saltwater Crocodile (Crocodylus Porosus)

Eastern Spotted Quoll sitting on log - Tasmania, Australia.

SPOTTED QUOLL

The spotted quoll is native to Australia and is also a marsupial, like the koala and kangaroo. It lives in wet forests. This unusual animal has red-brown fur with distinct white spots. Its tail is almost as long as the length of its head and body. It has ridged pads on its feet that allow it to easily climb up trees. During the day, it rests in its den, but at night it hunts snakes, small birds, and lizards to eat.

Tasmanian endemic endangered spotted quoll.

Australian Wombat(vombatus ursinus).

WOMBAT

The wombat is a large and rather pudgy mammal. Wombats dig extensive tunnels with chambers underground. These burrows are in eucalyptus forests and grasslands. They are marsupials, but unlike the others, their pouches face their rear ends so that dirt won't get in there while they are digging. Wombats have large incisors that don't stop growing.

Like rodents, they must gnaw on tree bark to wear them down. Wombats have the driest poop of any mammal. Even though they have a round opening like other animals, their poop comes out in cubes! If a wombat feels threatened, it will run to its burrow and close the entrance with its powerful rear end. If the attacker still tries to get in, the wombat crushes the intruder's skull with its rear.

Wombat spotted during the day. Tasmania, Australia.

Awesome! Now you know more about some of the unique animal life in Australia and Oceania. You can find more Explore the World books from Baby Professor by searching the website of your favorite book retailer.

Wombat walking on grassland.

Visit

BABY PROFESSOR
EDUCATION KIDS

www.BabyProfessorBooks.com

to download Free Baby Professor eBooks
and view our catalog of new and exciting
Children's Books

Made in United States
Troutdale, OR
03/31/2024

18853709R00040